Eleven Movie Songs

Arranged by CARL STROMMEN

Jazz-Style Arrangements

CONTENTS

Project Manager/Editor: Thom Proctor
Production Coordinator: Karl Bork
Art Design: Thais Yanes
Engraver: Mark Burgess
CD Producer: Teena Chinn
Recording Engineer: Kendall Thomsen
Recorded at Starke Lake Studios

Flute, Clarinet, Alto Sax, Tenor Sax: Jeff Rupert
Trumpet: Tom Macklin
F Horn: Kathy Gabriel
Trombone: Jeff Thomas
Piano and Keyboards: Teena Chinn
Guitar: Lindsay Blair
Bass: Charles Archard
Drums and Percussion: Keith Wilson

2
TROMBONE
SWEET GEORGIA BROWN
Words and Music by
BEN BERNIE, MACEO PINKARD
and KENNETH CASEY
Arranged by CARL STROMMEN
Full Track 2
Accompaniment Track 3
Bright jazz ♩ = 176
In 2
In 4
F6
E7
E♭7
mf
D7
G7
C7
F
Gm7
A♭dim7
F/A
F6
Em7
A7
D7
G7
A7
Dm7
Em7
A7
Dm7
Em7
A7
© 1925 WARNER BROS. INC. (Renewed)
All Rights Reserved including Public Performance
0709B

3
To Coda
D.S. al Coda
To Coda
0709B

OVER THE RAINBOW

Music by HAROLD ARLEN
Lyric by E.Y. HARBURG
Arranged by CARL STROMMEN

Am7(♭5) D7(♭9) Gm7 A7(♭5) A♭(9) Am7(♭5) D7
Gm7 C7(♭9) Fm7 D♭9 E♭maj7 C7(♭9)
Fm7 E7 E♭6 Fm9 B♭13 Am7(♭5) D7(♭9)
Gm7 A7(♭5) A♭maj7 Am7(♭5) D7 Gm7 C7(♭9)
Fm7 B♭9 E♭maj7 C9 F13 B♭9 E♭6 A♭/B♭
E♭maj7/B♭ Fm7/B♭ Dm7/G C13 Fm9 E7(♯9)
E♭maj7/B♭ Am7(♭5) D7(♭9) D7 Gm7 F♯dim7 Fm7 B♭9
Am7(♭5) D7(♭9) Gm7 A7(♭5) A♭(9) B♭9
Gm7 C7(♭9) A♭maj7 B♭9 E♭maj7 C7(♭9)
F13 B♭9 D♭9 E♭
D.S. al Coda Coda
Fm7 E7(♯9) E♭maj7
mf mp mp ritard.

A DAY IN THE LIFE OF A FOOL

7
Am7   Bm7(4) E7   Am7   Dm7   G9   C6
C#dim7   Dm7   G9   Cmaj7   Fmaj7
Bm7(b5)   E7   Am7   E7
57 Am7   Bm7(b5)   E7(b9)   Am7   Bm7(b5)   E7
Em7(b5)   A7(b9)   Dm7   C#dim7
Dm   Dm/C   Bm7(b5)   E7   Am   Am/G   Fmaj7   (loco)
Bm7   E7   Am7   Bm7(b5)   E7
Am   Dm7   Em7   Fmaj7   Em7
3   3   3   3
Dm7   Em7   Am   G/A Am   Fmaj7   G/F Fmaj7
3   3   mf   mp
F Em7 Fmaj7   Em7   Dm7   Em7   Am   G   Am
p
0709B

BYE, BYE, BLACKBIRD

9
0709B

AS TIME GOES BY

DAYS OF WINE AND ROSES

Gm7
Bbm7
Eb9
Am7
Am7/D
Dm7
Gm7
Em7
A7
Dm9(4)
Dm7
G13
G7
Gm7
C7(b9)
53 Fmaj7
Eb9
D
Em7
Fdim7
D/F#
Gm7
Bbm7
Eb9
Am7
Dm7
Bm7(no5th)
Bb7(#11)
Am7
Dm7
Gm7
C9
Am7
D7(b9)
Gm9
Bm7(b5)
Bbm7
Am7(#5)
Ab13
Gm7
C11
F6

EMILY

Full Track 14
Accompaniment Track 15
Music by JOHNNY MANDEL
Words by JOHNNY MERCER
Arranged by CARL STROMMEN
Gently - hold back ♩ = 92 (even eighths)
rubato
(a tempo)
mp
Cmaj9
Am9
Am7/D
G7(13)
G9
C6
B♭maj7/C
C7(♭9)
F(9)
F§
B♭13
B♭9
Amaj7
F#m7
Bm7
D/E
E7(♭9)
Am7
D9
Dm7
G7(#5)
Cmaj7
Am7
Dm9
G13
G9
Cmaj9
B♭maj7/C
Fmaj9
F6
E7(#9)
E7(♭9)
Am7
B9
Em7
A9
Dm7
G13
Em7(♭5)
A7
Dm7
Fm§
Em7

0709B

0709B

THE WAY YOU LOOK TONIGHT

MISTY

Music by ERROLL GARNER
Arranged by CARL STROMMEN

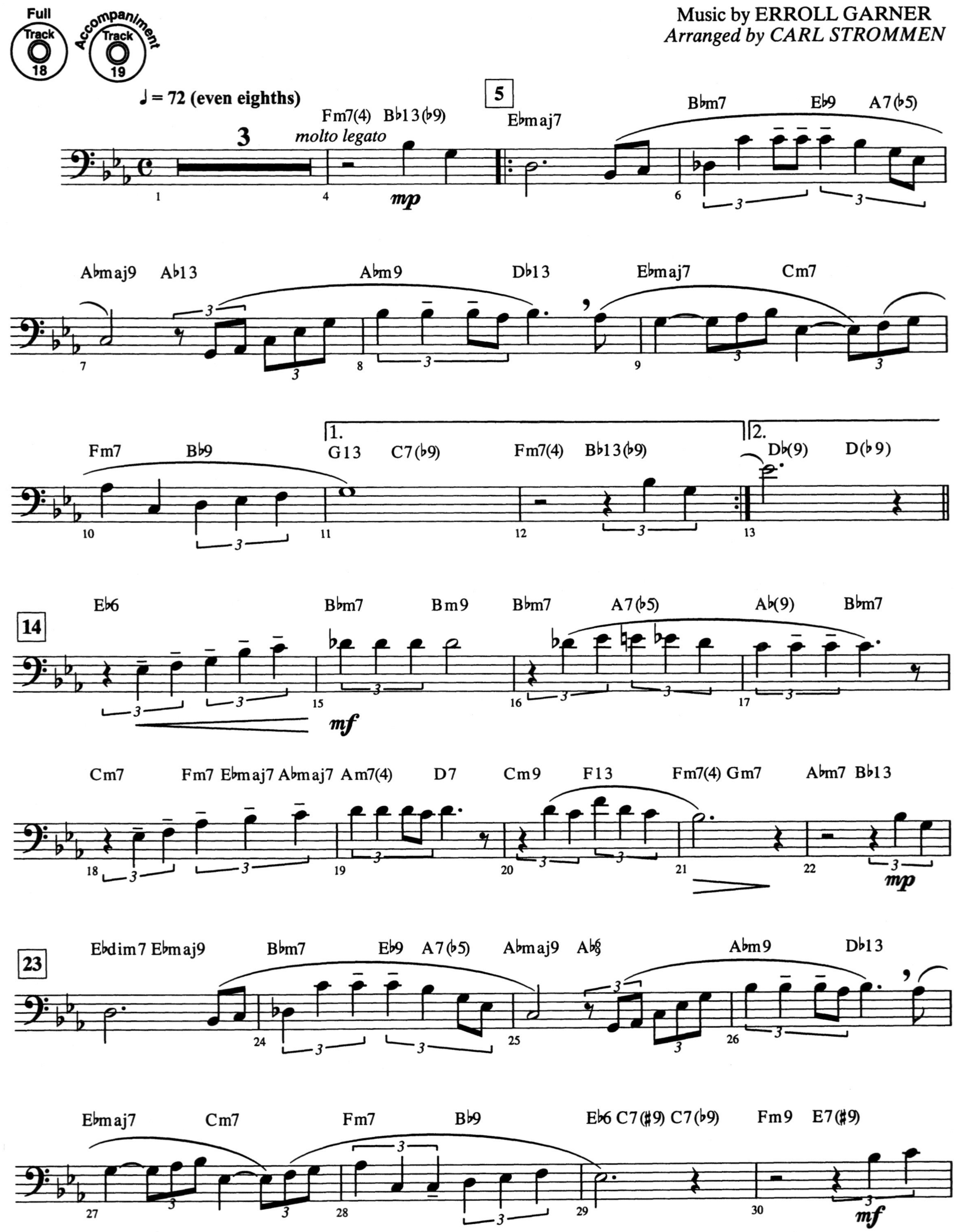

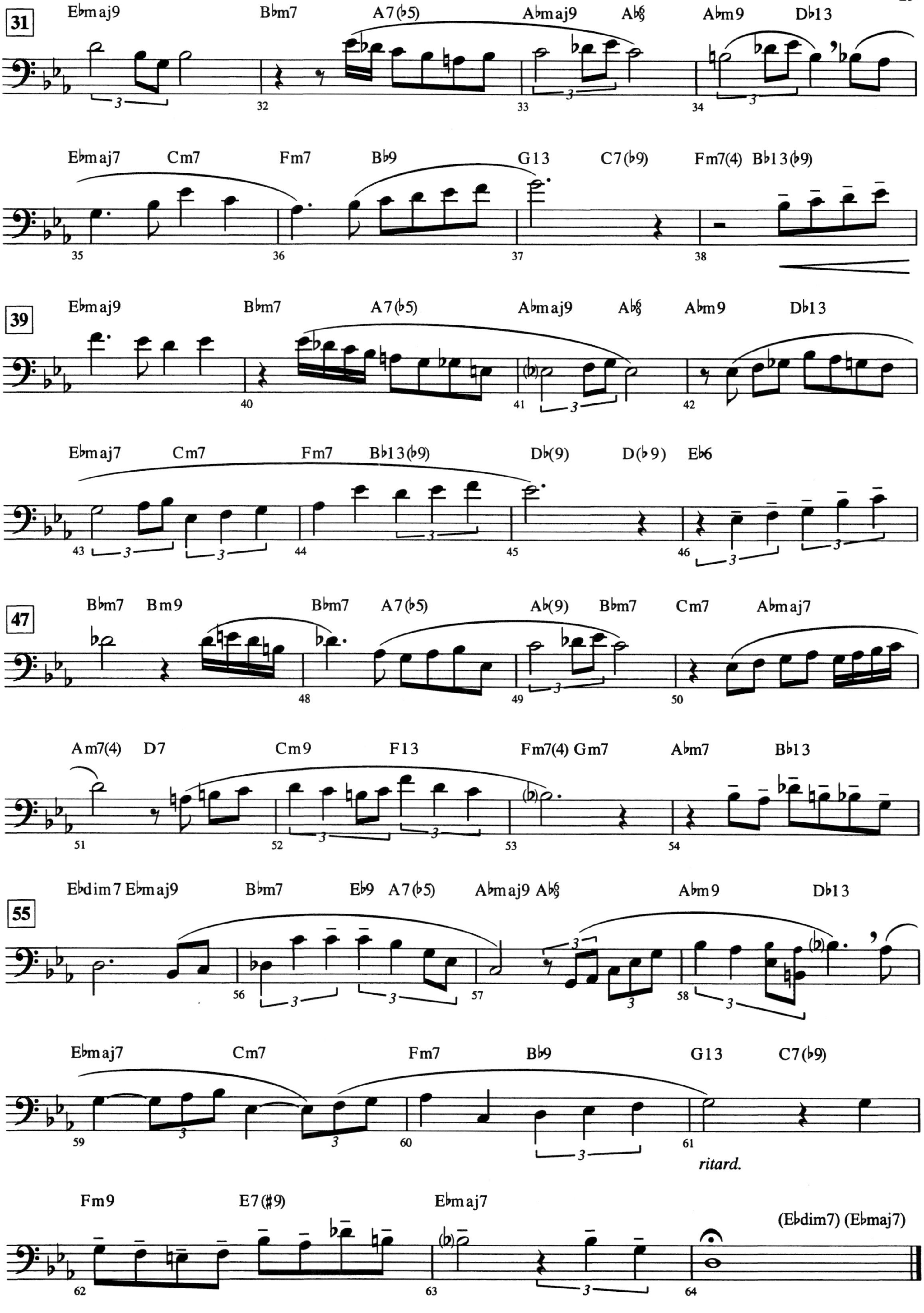
31
Ebmaj9 Bbm7 A7(b5) Abmaj9 Ab6/9 Abm9 Db13
Ebmaj7 Cm7 Fm7 Bb9 G13 C7(b9) Fm7(4) Bb13(b9)
39
Ebmaj9 Bbm7 A7(b5) Abmaj9 Ab6/9 Abm9 Db13
Ebmaj7 Cm7 Fm7 Bb13(b9) Db(9) D(b9) Eb6
47
Bbm7 Bm9 Bbm7 A7(b5) Ab(9) Bbm7 Cm7 Abmaj7
Am7(4) D7 Cm9 F13 Fm7(4) Gm7 Abm7 Bb13
55
Ebdim7 Ebmaj9 Bbm7 Eb9 A7(b5) Abmaj9 Ab6/9 Abm9 Db13
Ebmaj7 Cm7 Fm7 Bb9 G13 C7(b9)
ritard.
Fm9 E7(#9) Ebmaj7 (Ebdim7) (Ebmaj7)

ON GREEN DOLPHIN STREET

D7/C
Dbmaj7/C
C6/9
53 Swing
Dm11
G7(b13#9)
G7(b13b9)
Cmaj9
Fm11
Bb13
Bb13(b9)
Ebmaj7
Dm11
G7
61 Latin
C6/9
Cm9
D7/C
Dbmaj7/C
C6/9
69 Swing
Dm11
Bm7(b5) E7
Am9
Am/G
F#m7(b5) B7
Em7 Am7
Dm7 G13
75 Latin
Cm9
D7/C
Dbmaj7/C
C6/9
Swing
Dm7
Bm7(b5) E7
Am9 Am/G
F#m7(b5) B7
Em11 A7
Dm11 G13
89 Latin
C6/9
2

ALMOST LIKE BEING IN LOVE

45
Ebmaj9
F13
Bbmaj9
G13
46
47
48
Cm7
F13
Bb13 A13(b9) Fm11
Bb13
49
50
51
52
3
Ebmaj7
F13
Bbmaj9
Dm11
G7
53
54
55
56
Cm7
F13
Bb
Cm7 C#dim7 Bb/D
57
58
59
60
f
Am7
D7
G
Am7
Bbdim7
G/B
61
62
63
64
Gm7
C9
Am7
D7
65
66
67
68
69
Ebmaj7
F13
Bbmaj9
Dm11
G7
70
71
72
Cm7
C#dim7
Bbmaj7/D
Edim7
73
74
75
76
D.S. % al Coda
Cm7
F13
Bb13
A13(b9) Ab13
Fm11 Bb13
77
78
79
80
Coda
Cm9
F13
Ebmaj7 Dm7 Cm7 Bbmaj7
81
82
83
84

HOW TO USE THIS BOOK

Because of the great melodies and rich chord progressions, the music from movies continues to be fertile ground for jazz players. The transcribed solos have been slightly altered to conform to a moderate degree of difficulty. The player should use the written solo section as a guide and a springboard to personal improvising efforts.

The nuances of the jazz style are impossible to notate exactly. Key to this style is the concept of the swing or syncopated rhythm. The treatment and interpretation of eighth notes largely contribute to this elusive feel. In rock or Latin style music, eighth notes are played as written, evenly, with the accent on the downbeat:

Swing eight notes are treated differently at different tempos, but they are always written as even eighths. At moderate tempos the figure would be played as . At bright tempos, the swing feel tends to flatten out and is played more evenly with the pulse on the second half of the beat: .

Slower tempos (ballads) also tend to have a slightly more even eighth note feel. (Notice in listening to some solos that although the rhythm section is playing in a 12/8 feel, the solo is being played with even eighth notes.)

Players who are used to playing only in orchestral or wind ensemble settings have to make the adjustment of observing and interpreting eighth notes differently when placed in a big band or small group environment.

Some of the following unique jazz articulations are written out in these arrangements, but you can add more, tastefully, to create your own style.

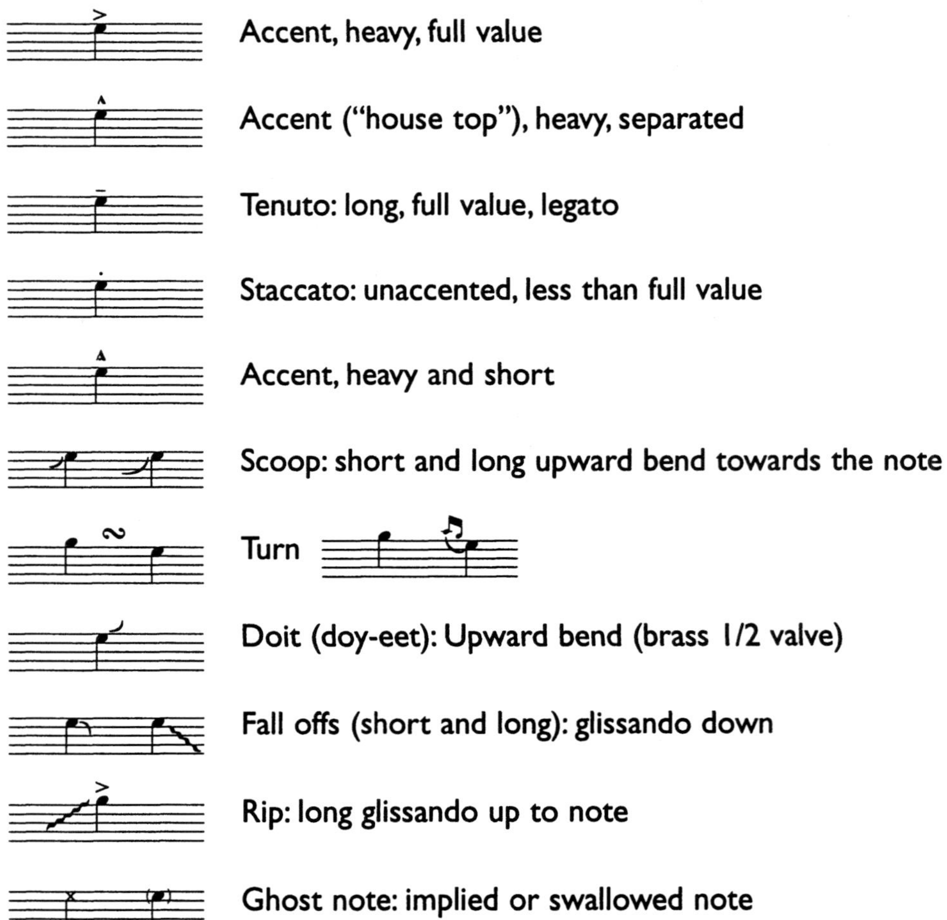

Accent, heavy, full value

Accent ("house top"), heavy, separated

Tenuto: long, full value, legato

Staccato: unaccented, less than full value

Accent, heavy and short

Scoop: short and long upward bend towards the note

Turn

Doit (doy-eet): Upward bend (brass 1/2 valve)

Fall offs (short and long): glissando down

Rip: long glissando up to note

Ghost note: implied or swallowed note

Also available: *Gershwin® By Special Arrangement* and *Broadway By Special Arrangement,* arranged by Carl Strommen.

For more information and further study of improvisation, refer to the Jazz Improvisation Series books *Approaching the Standards* by Dr. Willie L. Hill, Jr., published by Warner Bros. Publications.